SACAJAWEA

SACAJAWEA

Olive Burt

A Visual Biography

*Illustrated with
authentic prints
and documents*

*Franklin Watts
New York / London / 1978*

Original maps by Vantage Art, Inc.
Photo research by Selma Friedman
Cover design by Rafael Hernandez

Library of Congress Cataloging in Publication Data

Burt, Olive Wooley, 1894–
  Sacajawea.

  (A Visual biography)
  Includes bibliographical references and index.
  SUMMARY: A biography of the Shoshoni Indian
woman who acted as an interpreter, nurse, and
guide for the Lewis and Clark expedition.
    1. Sacagawea, 1786–1884—Juvenile literature.
2. Shoshoni Indians—Biography—Juvenile literature.
3. Scouts and scouting—The west-Biography—
Juvenile. 4. Lewis and Clark Expedition—Juvenile
literature. [1. Sacagawea, 1786–1884. 2. Shoshoni
Indians—Biography. 3. Indians of North America—
Biography. 4. Lewis and Clark Expedition]
I. Title.
F592.7.S123B87   970'.004'97   [B] [92]   78–1572
ISBN 0–531–00975–0

A Note on the Illustrations

Included among the illustrations in this book are reproductions of actual entries in the journals written by Meriwether Lewis and William Clark during their expedition that describe events mentioned in this book. Many American artists of the nineteenth and early twentieth centuries were fascinated by the exploration of the West, and by Indian life. We have shown two paintings by Charles M. Russell, who was especially interested in the Lewis and Clark expedition.

———

THE SETTING

In 1800 Thomas Jefferson was elected the third President of the United States. At that time there were sixteen states in the Union, all of them east of the Mississippi River. West of that river were only scattered settlements and Indian country. The entire vast region drained by the Missouri River, more than 2,300 miles (3,700 km) long, was known as the Louisiana Territory, claimed by France. Beyond the Rockies, the land was chiefly under Spanish control with the Northwest disputed by England, Russia, Spain, and the United States.

From the Mississippi to the Rocky Mountains stretched a rich region, fed by rushing rivers, sheltered by mountains, shadowed by forests, or shimmering with grassy plains. In the East people began looking toward this abundant storehouse of nature's gifts. They began thinking of taking advantage of those riches for themselves. Thomas Jefferson was one who looked toward the West, not for himself, but for the young nation. He was convinced that the United States should extend from the Atlantic to the Pacific. The first step must be the acquiring of the land west of the Mississippi, where Napoleon had hoped to establish a French empire.

Across the Atlantic, Napoleon was trying to conquer all Europe. Facing the conflict with England, he decided he could not also protect his American holdings, which he had just wrested from Spain. He decided to sell this land to the United States rather than lose it. A bargain was struck, with the United States paying

Napoleon twelve million dollars for the entire Louisiana Territory. It also promised to pay any claims the settlers had against the French government. These amounted to some three million dollars.

It was a tremendous bargain. For fifteen million dollars the United States had not only gained a wide, rich region, but had also won complete control of the Mississippi River. But neither the President nor the American people knew exactly what they had obtained. It was necessary to learn just what lay between the Mississippi and the Rockies, and what would be found beyond those shining mountains.

Even before the bargain with France had been made, President Jefferson had been considering a plan to send an expedition into the Northwest to learn about the people and resources and to discover whether there was a waterway across the continent. Near St. Louis the mighty Missouri emptied into the Mississippi, which flowed down to the Gulf of Mexico. If a usable water route could be found from the headwaters of the Missouri across to the Columbia River, which emptied into the Pacific, the Americans would have a way to reach the Orient, which lay beyond that ocean. Trade with the Orient would enrich the young nation. At the same time, the expedition could determine whether the Northwest region was suitable for settlement. Now there was even more reason for such an expedition, and President Jefferson sent one out.

The exploring party was led by two officers of the regular army. Meriwether Lewis was the official captain but he accorded equal rank and authority to his fellow officer, William Clark. The expedition left St. Louis on May 14, 1804. It went up the Missouri into what is now North Dakota, and spent the winter among the Mandan Indians who lived along the river. In the spring the party continued its journey, reaching the Pacific in November. The explorers spent the winter on the coast, return-

Meriwether Lewis

William Clark

ing the next spring up the Columbia and down the Missouri to St. Louis. They arrived there on September 23, 1806, two years and four months after their departure.

They did not find the waterway they sought but they did learn a great deal about the country, its climate, people, and animals. And their presence in the Northwest at that particular time strengthened the United States' claim to that region.

In order to find a route between the headwaters of the Missouri and the Columbia, the men had to cross the Rocky Mountains. This section of their journey required horses to carry supplies and men. The horses would have to be purchased from the Shoshone Indians who inhabited that region. Since the explorers did not speak or understand the Shoshone language, they needed an interpreter to go with them and help them in bargaining with the Indians. At their camp on the Upper Missouri they found such an individual—a young Shoshone woman, perhaps only sixteen or seventeen years old, who had been kidnapped from her tribe some five years before the advent of the expedition. This was Sacajawea.

Her story has been the subject of dispute among the historians who have attempted to reconstruct it. Indians kept no written record of what happened to them, but they took great pride in preserving their history through oral accounts, and scholars have found such accounts to be remarkably dependable.

Sacajawea's story, as told in this book, depends largely on the research done by Dr. Grace R. Hebard, former Wyoming State historian, who spent thirty years searching out and verifying, so far as was possible, the details of the life of this remarkable woman. Much of Dr. Hebard's final story depended on an "educated guess" as to what happened. Unless such details have been supported by other evidence, they will be treated here as what they were—a "guess." Other histories and journals have provided details discovered after Dr. Hebard published her work.

UP THE MISSOURI

The spring of 1805 came reluctantly to Fort Mandan, huddled on the bank of the Missouri River in what is now North Dakota. But it came at last, releasing the ice-bound canoes and opening the river to travel. Suddenly the fort was alive with activity as the men made ready to continue the journey which had been interrupted by the coming of winter. Nearby, in the clustered villages of Mandan and Minnetaree, the joyful Indians were greeting spring with ritual ceremonies. Now separated from her former neighbors, but rejoicing with them, was Sacajawea, a young woman of the Snake tribe, here far from her home in the Rocky Mountains.

Sacajawea had spent the winter at Fort Mandan. It had been a time of adjustment for the young woman, scarcely more than a girl—adjustment from the free life she had known to the rigors of a military camp. For Fort Mandan was just that, a camp established under military officers to shelter the members of an expedition sent out by President Thomas Jefferson to explore America's newly acquired territory and to discover, if possible, a water route to the Pacific. This meant tracing the Missouri to its source, then crossing the mountains that separate the far west from the eastern and mid-western areas of the continent. On the far side of this Great Divide, they were to learn whether the Columbia River could be reached by water and whether the Indians along the river would permit its use.

The expedition was commanded by two army officers, Captain Meriwether Lewis and his companion, William Clark.

Left: Sacajawea
Below: drawing
of Lewis and
Clark holding
a council with
the Indians.

They knew that the Missouri had its source in the land of the Shoshones. To cross the mountains they would have to purchase horses from those Indians. But no member of the expedition knew anything about the Shoshones, nor could anyone speak their language. The officers had been uncertain what to do until they learned that Toussaint Charbonneau, a French Canadian they had engaged to act as interpreter among the river tribes, had two wives who had been kidnapped from the Snake Indians, or Shoshones.

The officers had interviewed the two women and had chosen Sacajawea, the younger of the two, to teach them the customs and the language of her people. Finding her knowledge helpful, they had engaged her to accompany the expedition, to act as interpreter and go-between in the bargaining for horses. Sacajawea and her husband, with his other wife, called Otter Woman by many writers, had been quartered in the fort during the winter. This made it easy for Lewis and Clark to hold long sessions with the woman.

At first the conferences were difficult and tedious. Usually George Drewyer, as the officers called Drouillard, a French Canadian and the official interpreter for the expedition, was brought in to help. The captains would ask a question in English, the only language they knew; Drewyer would repeat this in French for Charbonneau, who would then translate it into the jargon used in his family—a mixture of French, Minnetaree, and Shoshone, emphasized by gestures, oaths, and even blows. However, Charbonneau restrained his impatience during these sessions, his responses modified by the attitude of the officers. They treated the young wife with respect and courtesy that acted as a silent warning to her husband.

Sacajawea had found the military life strange and rigorous, but she had adapted to it. She learned to waken at bugle call, to eat her meals at definite times each day, to observe rules set

OREGON

Fort Clatsop

Columbia R.

Missouri R.

Great Falls

Three Forks   Yellowstone R.   Mandan   Fort Mandan
                                  Villages   Fort
                                              Clark

Fort Manue

Natural

Fort Boise

Boundary

Continental

Divide

Missouri R.

Shoshone
Reservation

LOUIS

Fort Bridger

Virginia City

Auburn

SPANISH

Fort St. Vrain
Fort Lupton

Bent's Fort

Continental Divide

PU

POSSESSIONS

Pacific
Ocean

Mission
San Luis Rey

Natural Boun

A MAP OF
UNITED STATES IN 1804
Also showing places connected with
SACAJAWEA
The Bird Woman and her family

━━━ Lewis and Clark's Route to the Pacific
▪▪▪▪ Lewis and Clark's Return Route

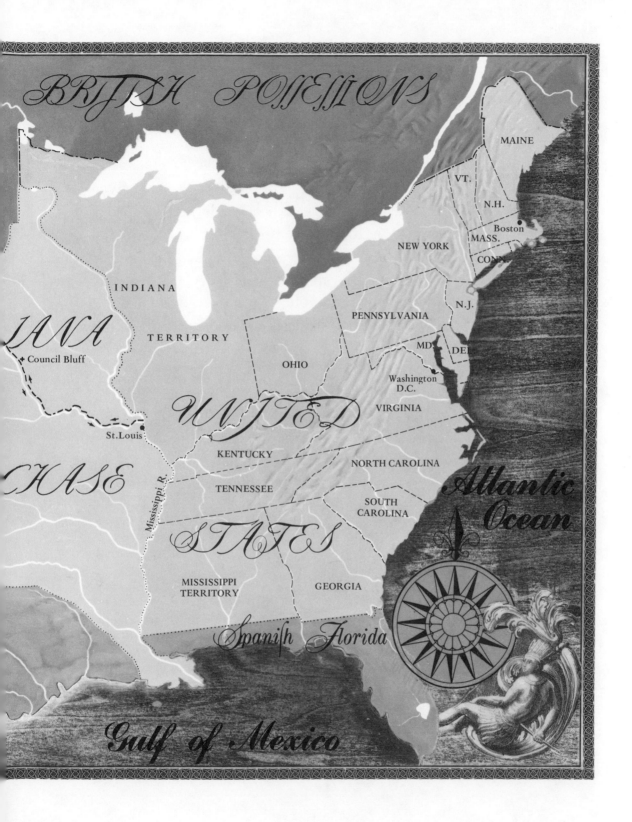

BRITISH POSSESSIONS

MAINE

VT.

N.H.

Boston

MASS.

NEW YORK

CONN.

N.J.

INDIANA

PENNSYLVANIA

TERRITORY

MD.

DEL.

OHIO

Washington
D.C.

IANA

VIRGINIA

Council Bluff

UNITED

St.Louis

KENTUCKY

NORTH CAROLINA

CHASE

TENNESSEE

Atlantic
Ocean

SOUTH
CAROLINA

STATES

Mississippi R.

MISSISSIPPI
TERRITORY

GEORGIA

Spanish Florida

Gulf of Mexico

by others, whereas before her needs and desires had been the guiding principles of her life. She admired the captains, though she was somewhat in awe of Lewis, a silent, brooding man. Clark was easier to get along with: his friendly blue eyes, flaming red hair, and ever-cheerful manner won the admiration and loyalty of whites and Indians alike.

On the afternoon of February 11 Sacajawea had given birth to a son, her first child. It had been a difficult delivery, during which Lewis had been persuaded to contribute two rattle-snake rattles, which had been powdered and dropped into a mug of water that Sacajawea drank as an aid to her struggle. Recording this event in his journal, Lewis wrote: "Whether this medicine was truly the cause or not I shall not undertake to determine, but I was informed that she had not taken it more than ten minutes before she brought forth."

Sacajawea called the husky little fellow Pomp—a Shoshone word meaning head or leader, often applied to a first son. Captain Clark often called him Pompey, seeming to make a good-natured reference to the great Roman soldier as an ideal for the child. Charbonneau, however, objected to the name, possibly because he already had a son, or sons, older than this baby. This supposition is supported by the fact that he did not name the boy Toussaint after himself, as he would normally name a first son. Instead, the baby was formally named Jean Baptiste. In later years a Toussaint Charbonneau appeared, a boy a few years older than Sacajawea's son, and accepted by many historians as Pomp's half-brother.

The baby, now two months old, was strapped into a cradle-board on his mother's back, as she took her place in the flotilla that was forming that Sunday afternoon of April 7, 1805. She had been assigned a place in the bottom of the white pirogue. This was the largest of the canoes and would lead the others up the river. There she was exposed to the sun and had little room to move about, surrounded as she was by bales of trade goods, stacks of pelts and blankets, chests of medical supplies, canisters of powder, record books, and journals—all the precious baggage that would sustain them on their journey, pay for horses, and preserve a record of their activities.

At the stern of this large canoe a platform had been built with an awning overhead. Here, protected from the glaring sun, the two captains would sit, with Clark's black servant York and Lewis's dog, Scannon, at their feet. Charbonneau, Drewyer, Cruzatte (the head boatman, whose fiddling enlivened many an hour), and several other members of the party were also traveling in this canoe.

It was four o'clock in the afternoon before the canoes got underway. Sacajawea sat silent amid the noise of departure—Indians running along the riverbank, shouting farewells, voyagers singing, laughing, yelling responses to the Indians. She must have felt all the jubilation her companions were voicing, but her excitement was tempered by a sense of responsibility. Not only was she returning to her people after five years of captivity, but she felt that somehow she had been chosen to be the salvation of those people. They were poor and powerless against the marauding tribes which had received guns and ammunition from the British. The Snakes, isolated in the mountains, had no such weapons. Their bows and arrows were of no avail against armed raiders. But if she could serve the expedition, perhaps the Great Father in Washington would see to it that her people received the guns they needed. Yes, and woolen blankets, iron kettles, pins and knives, and all the other rewards that had given their enemies such power. Sacajawea felt this responsibility, though she had no words with which to express it, even to herself. All she knew, sitting there among the singing voyagers, was that she—and only she—had been chosen. She would do whatever she could.

The second day out she unexpectedly discovered one way

Interpreters, George Drewyer and Tausant Charbono, also a Black Man by the name of York, servant to Capt. Clark, an Indian Woman Wife to Charbono with a young child, and a Mandan Man who had promised us to accompany us as far as the Snake Indians with a view to bring about a good under-standing and friendly intercourse between that na-on and his own, the Minetares and Ahwahharway.

Our vessels consisted of six small canoes, and two large perogues. This little fleet altho' not quite so respectable as those of Columbus or Capt. Cook, were still viewed by us with as much pleasure as those deservedly famed adventurers ever beheld theirs; and I were says with quite as much anxiety for their safety and pres-ervation. we were now about to penetrate a country at least two thousand miles in width, on which the foot of civillized man had never trodden; the good or evil it had in store for us was for experi-ment yet to determine; and these little vessells con-tained every article by which we were to expect to subsist or defend ourselves. however as the the state of mind in which we are, generally gives the colouring to events, when the immagination is

This entry in Lewis's journal mentions
"an Indian woman wife"—Sacajawea.

she could serve. Wanting something to enliven the meat and bread, she went poking through piles of driftwood around their camp. And she found what she was looking for—an abandoned nest left by wild mice. Stowed away there was a pile of dried roots, wild artichokes, left by the animals. Sacajawea gathered the roots, washed and boiled them. She offered some to the captains, who hesitated to eat the strange food, but when they overcame their hesitancy they discovered that here was something that might take the place of the potatoes they could not carry with them. Captain Lewis called the roots "wild artichokes" and found them similar to the Jerusalem artichokes of the South. These roots of a wild sunflower were used as a vegetable by southern country folk.

From that day on, Sacajawea often searched the ground for other edible plants to make their monotonous meals more palatable. She was the first to see the tender shoots of wild onions pushing up into the sunlight. As summer came she found wild strawberries, currants, plums, and choke-cherries. While Sacajawea probably wished only to be of service and was unaware of the true value of her contribution, she was supplying the vitamins that helped to keep the company fairly healthy though their diet was generally limited to meat and bread or flour pudding.

Whenever possible, many of the expedition walked along the shore. This not only eased the work of the rowers or tow-men; it provided exercise and was a welcome change from the cramped positions in the canoes. Captain Lewis liked to walk alone, with only Scannon for company. But Captain Clark enjoyed human companionship. Though York was always close by, the red-haired leader often invited Sacajawea and her husband to walk with him. He would ask the Shoshone to name strange plants or to identify a moccasin print, so fresh that they knew Indians were hovering about, though they were never seen. As the weeks passed this companionship became true friendship, and communication between the two became easy and spontaneous.

Wherever she went, Sacajawea carried Pomp in his snug blanket on her back. The journals say little about the baby, but when he is mentioned it is with an undertone of friendliness. Nowhere is there any complaint against the baby. Captain Clark, walking with the child's parents, grew very fond of the good-natured youngster.

It was a peaceful journey, much less exciting than anyone had anticipated. There were encounters with bears and panthers, rattlesnakes and angry buffalo. These provided excitement and topics of conversation. The greatest annoyance came from rain and dust storms, mosquitoes and gnats. Sacajawea protected her baby as well as she could, but sometimes his face was mottled, his eyes puffed shut from mosquito stings.

Then, one day in May, a sudden squall tipped the white pirogue almost over on its side. Charbonneau, who was steering, dropped the helm and began calling on God to save him. The pirogue was saved from a complete capsize by the awning at the stern. From the shore, Lewis and Clark watched with horror, unable to make the struggling men on board hear their shouts and commands. The efforts of the men with the sails righted the vessel, but it had taken in a great deal of water, which now sloshed about and over the gunwale. The splashing water picked up everything that was light enough to float, threatening to carry it overboard to be lost forever. Many of the most important supplies had been entrusted to this large canoe: medicines, seeds, trade goods, the journals and accounts of the journey. But the attention of the men was all on righting the canoe, and the captains were helpless.

Sacajawea kept her head, quietly and efficiently reaching out and catching the floating objects, preventing their loss. Lewis, recording the event in his journal, praised the Indian woman for

*This romantic mural shows the
expedition on the Columbia River.*

her fortitude and resolution, which had preserved so much of the
threatened supplies and made their losses much less than they
had feared.

A few days later the flotilla passed a handsome stream, which
Lewis named the "Sah-cah-gar-we-ah" (as he pronounced and
spelled her name) in honor of her quick action in saving their
supplies. This is one of the few times Sacajawea was mentioned
by name in any of the journals kept by members of the expedition.
She was usually referred to as "our interpreter's wife," "our
Indian woman," or simply "the squar" (squaw). Clark called
her Jane or Janey, claiming that he could neither pronounce nor
spell her Indian name.

In later years, when discussion of the Shoshone's name became popular, that entry in Captain Lewis's diary would prove that she was using this, her Minnetaree name, while traveling with the expedition. Charbonneau had explained that the name meant "bird woman," a romantic term which has clung to her through the years, though some authorities claim that is a misinterpretation of the name. They claim it really means "boat launcher." Sacajawea had many names, as is customary among most Indian tribes. These will be discussed as they appear in this account of her life.

While the men suffered many ailments, cuts and bruises, colic, rheumatism, and so on, neither Sacajawea nor her baby seem to have been ill until June, when the Shoshone was stricken with a mysterious ailment that mystified and worried the officers. Soon after she first took sick, Captain Lewis went off on an exploring jaunt. Captain Clark tried every medication he could think of. But doses of salts, poultices of hot pine bark, even bloodletting had no effect.

When Lewis returned and found that their usual treatments were useless, he decided to try mineral water from a spring he had passed on the other side of the river. A canoe was sent to obtain that water, which Lewis ordered to be the only thing Sacajawea should take for awhile. It worked. Almost immediately she felt better. She suffered a setback when Charbonneau allowed her to eat some Indian breadfruit and dried fish, which caused her great pain. Angry at the Frenchman's carelessness, for he had been warned that she must have nothing but liquids, Captain Lewis placed her again on the mineral water only and she soon recovered from the attack.

Clark's party of explorers was camped below the Great Falls of the Missouri River when this happened. Lewis had a camp above the falls. They would have to maintain the two posts while they portaged their canoes and baggage around the tremendous cataract. This would take them from June 21 to July 15, nearly a month of back-breaking labor. During that time Sacajawea had another narrow escape.

Captain Clark decided one morning to walk to the upper camp. He invited Sacajawea, her husband, and York to go with him. Soon after they reached the falls, Clark saw dark clouds, threatening a rainstorm. These storms came on suddenly, giving those on the ground little chance to escape a drenching. But nearby was a narrow canyon, with high walls that seemed to offer protection from the coming storm. The group hastened into the defile and under its sheltering walls Sacajawea laid Pompey naked on a blanket.

Suddenly a cloudburst further up the canyon sent a wall of water rushing down the narrow ravine. There was no time to escape the way they had come, and they could not remain where they were or they would surely be swept away by the torrent. The only escape was to climb the sheer walls to the canyon rim. York had already made his way to the top, and now Charbonneau started to scramble up, weeping and praying for deliverance. In vain Clark yelled at him to help his wife and child, but the Frenchman was so terrified he could do nothing. Sacajawea had snatched Pomp up from the blanket, and clutched him in her arms as she tried to scramble up the slippery rocks in the pelting rain. Clark, below her, half pushed, half pulled the struggling woman higher and higher, until they both fell, shaking and panting, over the rim to safety.

They had been terrified, but not really hurt, though they were cold and wet. Captain Clark feared this exposure would be dangerous to the Shoshone so soon after her illness. So she was kept warm and quiet until the canoes and baggage were all moved to the upper camp, ready to proceed on up the river to the mountains.

Sacajawea was excited as the canoes moved upstream. This

was her homeland; she kept recognizing landmarks, kept looking for a camp, or just a horseman, of her own people. Then, one morning, they emerged from a dangerous gorge onto a wide plain where three rivers met and joined to form the one on which they were traveling—the Missouri. Lewis and Clark named the three rivers the Jefferson, the Madison, and the Gallatin, but they had no idea which one would take them to the mountains and to the very source of the Missouri. After a good deal of discussion, speculation, and exploration of the surrounding territory, both leaders agreed to follow the Jefferson, which seemed most likely to have its source in the mountains they hoped to reach.

Sacajawea somberly regarded their camp there at the Three Forks of the Missouri. She was remembering what had happened five years before when she, with a group of Shoshones, had camped on this very spot. How she conveyed the information to the captains is not explained in the journals, but Lewis wrote a brief account of what had happened:

> *Our present camp is precisely on the spot that the Snake Indians were encamped at the time the Minnetares of the Knife R. first came in sight of them five years since. from hence they retreated about three miles up Jefferson river and concealed themselves in the woods. the Minnetares pursued, attacked them, killed 4 men, 4 women a number of boys, and made prisoners of all the females and four boys. Sah-cah-gar-we-ah* our Indian woman was one of *the female prisoners taken at that time; tho' I cannot discover that she shews immotion of sorrow in recollecting this event, or of joy in being restored to her native country; if she has enough to eat and a few trinkets to wear I believe she would be perfectly content anywhere.*

Sergeant John Ordway, who also kept a journal, wrote:

She tells us that she was taken in the middle of the River as she was crossing at a Shole place to make hir ascape.

This information is not much on which to reconstruct the childhood of this heroic woman, but enough to let us know that she was participating in the daily life of her people—a semi-nomadic life in which hunger, danger, and cold were the chief elements. Captain Lewis's judgment of the Bird Woman's feelings was probably not shared by Red Hair. The next day he walked with her along the riverbank, encouraging her to show the exact spots where incidents had occurred. Though she had been just a child of about twelve, she must have been keenly observant, even in her panic. At one place she saw ahead some oddly-shaped mountains. She pointed to them and explained that they were called Beaverhead Mountains by her people, who came there to collect red clay with which to paint their faces. Nearby was the pass the Snakes used to cross the mountains to their homeland on the other side.

Captain Lewis was impatient to reach the Snakes, buy horses, and get over the mountains before snow fell. He left the main party and with three companions set out across land in the hope of soon reaching his goal. Clark, suffering from a great tumor on his ankle, and the rest of the men continued up the river, which was becoming more difficult every day. The shallow water and the rapids made pulling the canoes difficult; the sharp rocks of the riverbed cut the men's feet; everyone was cold and wet and worn out.

To lighten the men's work as much as possible, those who were not rivermen walked along the shore. One day Sacajawea, with Pomp on her back, was walking with her husband and Captain Clark when they saw ahead of them a line of mounted Indians, surrounded by a crowd of women and children. Clark hesitated, not knowing what to expect. But Sacajawea gave one look at the horsemen and bounded forward, shrieking, dancing, whirling in delight. She stuck her fingers in her mouth to indicate that these were her people. A woman broke loose from the crowd and ran to embrace the newcomer. Then a horseman spurred forward and Clark recognized Drewyer, dressed and painted like an Indian. He had gone ahead with Lewis, but there was no sign of the captain. Now the entire band swept down upon Clark's men, embracing them as brothers, urging them with gestures and exclamations to hasten to the camp where the Shoshone chief awaited them. As they started forward Drewyer whispered to Clark that Captain Lewis had been in grave danger. Clark's arrival had proved that the expedition was, as Lewis had maintained, a friendly visit.

They had not gone far when they encountered the Shoshone chief, Cameâhwait, and his braves coming to meet them. And there was Lewis and his companions silently relieved to see the main party. A council was immediately set up, and Sacajawea was called in to interpret. This was the purpose of her long and difficult journey. But at the first words of the Shoshone chief, Sacajawea ran to him, weeping, and threw her blanket over his shoulder. She embraced the chief, while sobs shook her. Drewyer told Lewis this showed that Cameâhwait was the Bird Woman's brother. She opened the elkskin bag in which she kept her treasures and took out a lump of sugar. She had hoarded this as a treat for Pomp some day when he needed special comfort. Cameâhwait sucked on the lump, while he regarded his sister with emotion. And he promised to help her companions.

When the council ended, the women gathered around their long-lost "sister," welcoming her home. Her family were all gone save the chief and a brother who was away on a hunt. And there was a small nephew, the son of her dead sister. Sacajawea embraced the child and adopted him as her own.

S. 50. E. 1. to the entrance of a bold running stream
                    on Lard. side, distance by water 2 1/2 M.
                    at this place there is a very considerable
                    rapid and clift near on both sides
S. 45° W. 1/2 mile to the lower point of an Island
Miles 6 1/2 near the center of the Valley and river.

Saturday August 17th 1805.

This morning I arrose very early and dispatched
Drewyer and the Indian down the river. sent Sheilds
to hunt. I made McNeal cook the remainder of our
meat which afforded a slight breakfast for ourselves
and the Cheif. Drewyer had been gone about 2 hours
when an Indian who had straggled some little distance
down the river returned and reported that the whitemen
were coming, that he had seen them just below. they all
appeared transported with joy, & the chief repeated his fratir-
-nal hug. I felt quite as much gratifyed at this information as
the Indians appeared to be. Shortly after Capt. Clark ar-
-rived with the Interpreter Charbono, and the Indian wo-
-man, who proved to be a sister of the Chief Cameahwait.
the meeting of these people was really affecting, particular-
-ly between Sah cah-gar-we-ah and an Indian woman,
                                                                    with her,
who had been taken prisoner at the same time and who, had
afterwards escaped from the Minnetares and rejoined her nation. At Noon the Canoes arrived, and we had the satis-
-faction once more to find ourselves all together, with a
flattering prospect of being able to obtain as many
horses shortly as would enable us to prosicute our

*Meriwether Lewis's journal here
describes the reunion of "Sah-cah-gar-we-ah"
and her brother Cameâhwait.*

They were now at the eastern end of the trail over the Great Divide. The Shoshones here had few horses, but at the western village there were more animals. Sacajawea and several others set out for this village. There Sacajawea's knowledge of the people and their language helped the explorers to purchase nine horses, which were driven back over the pass for Lewis to use. The captain was so pleased with the woman's work that he had Charbonneau buy a horse for Sacajawea to ride. It was a disgrace to Charbonneau that his wife, a squaw, rode while he walked. The Indian women hired to carry baggage over the trail were as resentful as Charbonneau, but Sacajawea, with Pomp on her back, smiled disdainfully from her mount.

One night Sacajawea learned that her brother planned to withdraw his braves, who had been helping the explorers, and take them off on a buffalo hunt. Sacajawea was appalled. This would mean that the expedition, abandoned in the mountains in winter, would perish, their purpose unfulfilled. She urged Charbonneau to warn Captain Lewis, and after some argument, he did so.

Lewis called Cameâhwait into conference, accused him of treachery, and demanded that he abandon his scheme. The chief, subdued and remorseful, vowed he would keep his promises and help the expedition get over the mountains. Sacajawea's alertness, good sense, and loyalty had prevented a disaster.

TO THE PACIFIC
AND BACK

In the Snake village on the western slope of the Rocky Mountains, Captain Lewis waited impatiently for the return of Clark, who was out exploring the trail west. When Clark did return, the entire party was again together, with every member who had left Fort Mandan ready to go on to the Pacific. On August 29 they set out, but already the mountain passes were clogged with snow.

The horses stumbled and fell on the narrow, icy trails, threatening to slide to the bottom of the rocky canyon. Sacajawea could no longer carry Pomp on her back, but had to hold him in her arms, wrapped in her blanket and kept warm by her body, or he would freeze to death. He was now seven months old, a lively, husky child, whose wriggling in his blanket must have made his mother's task very difficult. None of the men had anything like this to contend with.

For nearly three weeks they fought the cold and snow of the mountain, and at last they came to the village of the friendly Chopunnish, or Nez Percés, the Pierced Noses. These people were very poor, but hospitable. They did all they could for the adventurers, many of whom were sick from exposure to wet and cold. Those who were well enough began making dugouts in which to travel down the Kooskooskee (Clearwater) and Snake to the Columbia. Their horses must be left here, but Twisted Hair, the Nez Percé chief, promised to care for the animals until their owners returned in the spring.

The black servant York was greatly admired by the Indians, who had probably never seen a black man before.

Sacajawea found that floating across the land that is now Idaho was much easier than managing a heavy baby and a stumbling horse on an icy trail. They met many bands of Indians, who treated them with friendliness though they had never before seen white men. Five canoes full of strange people were enough to awaken fear and hostility; trade goods and guns were a constant temptation to the roving bands. Captain Clark could not understand why they were not attacked until he learned that it was the presence of Sacajawea and Pomp that told the natives this was a friendly expedition. Captain Clark wrote in his journal: "A woman with a party of men is a token of peace."

And so, in mid-October they came to the banks of the Columbia. They made camp on a point of land that many years later would become the Sacajawea State Park of Washington. And again, it was Sacajawea's presence that guaranteed their safety. At first suspicious and wary, as soon as the Bird Woman appeared, the natives opened their lodges to the newcomers and shared their food with them.

The trip down the Columbia, though difficult because of the rapids, was rather uneventful. Then one evening the canoes began to bob up and down so violently that several of the party became seasick. They had reached the bay at the mouth of the river and the ocean tides were causing the disturbance.

It began to rain continually, hampering the search for a place to make their winter camp. Everyone, save Pomp, who was kept warm and dry by his mother, was wet and cold and dispirited. They had hoped to find a vessel sent by President Jefferson awaiting them for their return by sea. But no ship came. At last Captain Lewis found a firm meadow in a pine grove, and the men set to work building Fort Clatsop, named for a neighboring tribe of Indians.

Life at the fort was monotonous and wearying. Rain fell constantly. Sergeant Gass expressed in his journal what they all felt: "There is more wet weather on this coast than I ever knew in any place, during a month we have had but three fair days and there is no prospect of a change."

While the men hunted or made furniture or boiled salt from seawater, Sacajawea cared for Pomp, cooked, and sewed moccasins. During the winter she and two of the men who were clever with awls and strips of elk fashioned 338 pairs of moccasins. These made a great heap in a corner of a cabin. And during the long months Sacajawea began to develop from an inarticulate "squaw" into a forceful personality. The journals give glimpses of this change. Captain Clark wrote: "Squar displeased with me for not—" The unfinished sentence proves that the Bird Woman now dared show her displeasure, even with the friendly officer.

One day a Chinook chief came to the fort wearing a robe made of otter pelts. The captains had never before seen such beautiful fur and immediately coveted that robe. They offered various objects in exchange for it, but the only thing he would consider was the belt of blue beads which Sacajawea was wearing. This was her dearest possession and she refused to part with it. But finally, seeing how much the officers wanted the robe, she silently took off the belt and handed it to Captain Clark. He was jubilant, and the next day gave her a blue wool officer's coat. It would keep her warm, but it could not take the place of the treasured belt.

On Christmas Day, 1805, Sacajawea surprised Clark with a gift of two dozen white weasel tails from animals she had probably trapped. These would make elegant trimming for his leggings or vest. What the captain gave her is not recorded, nor do we know what she gave her son or her husband.

The ocean was not within sight of the camp, but from time to time some of the men went down to the shore to gaze upon the wondrous sight. Everyone except Sacajawea had made this trip, but no one had suggested that the Snake woman accompany a party. For some time Sacajawea evidently said nothing, but she must have resented this treatment. Then, soon after Christmas, news came that a whale had foundered on the shore some miles down the coast. The officers wanted some oil and blubber from the whale, and they also wished to see the strange animal. Captain Clark organized a party to go on the following Monday.

On Sunday the chosen men were discussing the coming adventure. Sacajawea listened awhile, then asked if she could go too. Both captains refused her request, but the Bird Woman persisted. She pointed out that she had shared the hardships and dangers of the journey and had come on from the Shoshone country for but one reason—to see the great waters. Now all save her had seen it. She alone had worked and suffered in vain. Now there was this new marvel, this monstrous fish. It seemed very hard on her to be left in camp while all the men went down to view it. She spoke so passionately that both captains agreed that she could go. This seems to be the only time that Sacajawea demanded recognition of her services.

Two days later the group, walking down the coast, came to a mountain which looked to be an impassable barrier. Some of the men turned back, but Sacajawea, with Pomp on her back, resolutely climbed the steep trail to the mountaintop, pulling herself up by grasping shrubs and clawing at rocks and bushes. There at the top, high above the beach, she gazed out at the vast expanse of ocean. She had never imagined such space. Her horizons had always been limited by mountains or forests. She took Pomp from her back and held him up to view the wonder. In later years he would claim that he could remember this, his first view of the ocean, but he was not yet a year old and his memory must have been helped by the stories his mother would have told him.

When at last Sacajawea descended to the beach she gave the whale a brief glance. It was just a bone-white skeleton now, all the blubber, oil, and meat carried away by the hungry Indians. The journals do not describe the Shoshone's reaction to this tremendous experience, but its effect on her must have been stupendous. Never again could she accept a world bounded by mountains—narrow, isolated, and restricted. Years later, her recollection of this day would help establish her identity as the real Bird Woman.

During the winter many of the men became sick. At one time Captain Clark became so ill he could not eat. He longed for some "plain bread." Sacajawea went to her parfleche—a skin bundle in which she carried her treasures—and took out a small package of flour. She had been saving this as a treat for Pomp, but she made it into a small loaf of "white man's bread." She gave this to the red-haired captain, who ate it with relish—although the first mouthful told him the morsel was slightly sour because the flour had gotten wet during the persistent rains. However, it was the first solid food he had been able to eat for days.

On March 23, 1806, the explorers said good-bye to the Pacific coast and its never-ending rainfall. The hoped-for ship to carry them home by sea and in comfort had never arrived. So they obtained canoes from the Clatsops and started back up the Columbia. It was not as pleasant as the downriver trip had been. Though most of the Indians were friendly, some were hostile, refusing to sell them food, hurling insults or even stones at the travelers.

All were glad to reach the friendly and hospitable Nez Percé, where they had to stop for awhile because the snow was still deep in the mountains and some of the men were too sick to travel. Here little Pomp, for the first time on the long journey, became very ill. He was teething and suffering from a sore throat and fever. For two weeks the captains worked over him and the whole party worried. The journals carried daily reports on the baby's condition. By June 3 the doses of salts, the hot poultices of wild onion, the gargling solutions began to work, and a week later Pomp was well enough to travel. By mid-June, though snow was still deep on the mountains in the passes it had melted enough to be traveled, and the party set out.

It was to be divided in order to explore more land. Captain Lewis, with a few men, would take a short cut to the Great Falls, to prove that there was a quicker, better route than the one they had taken last summer. Two or three men would drive the horses, now recovered from Twisted Hair. The rest would go with Captain Clark over their former trail, collecting the canoes and baggage that had been cached along the way. All would rendezvous on an island near the place where the Yellowstone entered the Missouri. From there they would proceed down the river to the Mandan villages.

Sacajawea was to be in the red-haired captain's party, and the next two weeks were probably the happiest of the Bird Woman's long life. Their route lay across fields of new grass, bright with spring flowers or looking like lakes of clear water where the blue camas flowers bloomed. Walking beside the captain and freed from the constraint she felt with Lewis, the Shoshone talked of her childhood. By now she could communicate with Clark without the clumsy translations by her husband.

When they came to the mountains, Sacajawea's remarkable memory made it possible for her to point out the passes and trails which her people had followed. It was here, and only here, that she acted as a guide. Clark wrote in his journal:

> *The Indian woman, who has been of great service to me as a pilot through this country, recommends a gap in the mountains more south which I shall cross.*

It was probably this statement which led early historians to conclude that the Bird Woman had guided the expedition through its entire journey. Thus she became known as the "guide for the Lewis and Clark expedition," which she was not.

Though they were in Snake territory, she did not see her brother again. Nor did she pick up the little nephew she had adopted. Why this was so the journals do not explain. It may have been that Sacajawea did not wish her personal affairs to intrude upon this idyllic interlude.

They wandered slowly, indulging in unhurried camps where Pomp could play in the grass while the men hunted or fished or loafed in the sunshine. When they reached the Yellowstone they made camp on the shore and the men began constructing canoes for the trip downriver. There was no hurry; they knew they would reach the rendezvous before the others. But finally they embarked in the new canoes and started down the Yellowstone. It was a happy trip, the only annoyance being the mosquitoes, which followed them in clouds of whirring wings and noxious stings.

There was one exciting break when they passed a strange rock formation rising from a meadow near the river. The canoes were beached, while the voyagers examined the rock. Captain Clark named it "Pomp's tower," for the little boy of whom he was so fond. Later it became known, as it is today, as Pompey's Pillar. Clark scratched his name and the date on one of the flat surfaces, among Indian drawings of horses and other animals. There it can be seen by today's travelers about halfway between Billings and Custer, Montana.

As they expected, they were at the rendezvous in time to greet the others as they arrived. The men entrusted with the horses came down the river in buffalo-skin bull boats. The Crows had stolen every horse. A few days later, Captain Lewis's group

*Painting by Charles Russell
depicts Lewis, Clark, and
Sacajawea, on the right, in Montana.*

arrived. And at sunrise the next day the reunited adventurers were skimming down the Missouri. With the wind at their backs they made excellent time. On the afternoon of the following day they reached the first Mandan village, shooting off their firearms, shouting and singing. They had done what no other white men had ever done: crossed and recrossed unknown country, met and lived with strange Indian tribes, collecting specimens of plants and animals unknown to the civilized world—and had not lost a single member. They had not found a waterway across the country, but they had proved that by boat or horse the continent could be traversed.

There was great rejoicing among the Indians as the explorers returned to pay a courtesy visit to the various chiefs and to retrieve any supplies left at Fort Mandan.

Sacajawea's actions were not recorded, but she probably made her way from the crowd to her husband's lodge to show off her wonderful son and to relate her adventures to the neighboring Indian women.

By Saturday, August 17, the captains had finished their business here. Sacajawea, with Pomp and Charbonneau, was in the crowd that gathered at the riverside to watch the white men depart for St. Louis. Charbonneau was paid $500.33 for his services as interpreter—the price of a horse and a lodge. Sacajawea was paid nothing, but Clark probably gave her a medal, the customary farewell gift to any Indian who had merited recognition. At any rate, years later her descendents searched for a medal they claimed their grandmother had worn. They also claimed that Clark had given her a brown leather wallet in which were papers that could prove her identity. Such a wallet was found, as will be told later, but its contents were so discolored by age and water they could not be deciphered.

Clark hated to leave his "dancing boy" and offered to take Pomp to St. Louis and rear him as his son. But the child was not

way that he had done. I offered to take his
little son a beautifull promising child who is
19 months old to which they both himself & wife
wer willing provided the child had been
weaned. they observed that in one year the boy
would be sufficiently old to leave his mother &
he would then take him to me if I could be
so friendly as to raise the child for him in
such a manner as I thought proper, to which
I agreed &c. — we droped down to the Beg white
Chief Mandan Village ½ a mile below on the
South Side, all the Indians proceeded on down
by land. and I walked to the lodge of the Chief
whome I found sorounded by his friends
the men were Setting in a circle Smokeing
and the woomin crying. he sent his bagage
with his wife & son, with the Interpreter
Jessonme & his wife and 2 children to the
Canoes provided for them. after smokeing
one pipe, and distributeing some powder &
lead which we had given him he informed
me that he was ready and we were accompd
to the Canoes by all the village many of them
cried out aloud. as I was about to shake
with the Grand Chiefs of all the villages there
assembled they requested me to set one
menut longer with them which I readily
acreed to and directed a pipe to be lit. the

*This journal entry outlines
William Clark's offer to raise Pomp.*

yet weaned and Sacajawea would not let him go. Clark wrote in his journal:

> *I offered to take his little son a butifull promising child who is 19 months old to which they both himself & wife were willing provided the child had been weened. they observed that in one year the boy would be suffiently old to leave his mother & and he would then take him to me if I would be so friendly as to raise the child for him in such a manner as I thought proper, to which I agreed &c.*

Captain Clark liked the Charbonneaus, even though the husband had sometimes annoyed him. He left his opinion to us:

> *This man has been very serviceable to us, and his wife particularly useful among the Shoshones. Indeed she has borne with a patience truly admirable the fatigues of so long a route encumbered with the charge of an infant, who is even now only nineteen months old.*

But the journal does not tell us what the captain said to the Bird Woman or to Pomp as he bade them good-bye, nor what she said to him. He climbed into his canoe, waved farewell, and was carried away by the river.

THE LOST YEARS

Captain Clark saying good-bye to Sacajawea, Charbonneau, and little Pomp is the last authentic reference to the Bird Woman by name so far as is known. For more than sixty years no mention is made of her in recognized journals, documents, or historical records. What happened to her during those years is a matter of speculation and dispute among those who have tried to unravel the mystery. As we examine the evidence that has been brought to light, we must bear in mind that Sacajawea was no longer the obedient, inarticulate girl she had been sixteen months before. She had sat in councils with white officers and Indian chieftains. She had been treated with respect by men beside whom her husband was an ignorant and brutish fellow. She could communicate with white men. Her mind had been opened to a world more vast than anything her sisters could know.

Most important of all, she had ridden a horse while her husband, a white man, went on foot. And she had a son, who even as a baby had proved to be a passport to unexpected privileges. At the end of the Pacific expedition, the Bird Woman was far more self-reliant and capable than others of her tribe. She, if anyone, could survive in that wild, unpredictable period in our history.

Whether she did survive has been a matter of discussion for many years. To put it simply: some historians claim that Sacajawea died at a trading post on the Upper Missouri on December 20, 1812; others are equally convinced that she died on the Shoshone Reservation in Wyoming on April 9, 1884. We cannot

Pacific Ocean

OREGON

Clark's Fork

Cape
Disappointment

Fort
Clatsop

Cascades

Columbia R.

Snake R.

Clearwater R.

Lolo Trail

BITTEROOT MTS.

Salmon R.

Lemhi R.

Snake R.

COUNTRY

A MAP OF
LEWIS AND CLARK'S EXPEDITION

Across Unexplored Wilderness of
<u>NORTH AMERICA</u>

Lewis and Clark's
◄— ◄— ◄— ◄ route to the Pacific
Lewis and Clark's
——→ ——→ return route
△ Camp ■ Fort ∧ Indian Village

Natural Boundary

SPANISH

Marias R.

Missouri R.

Great Falls

Judith R.

Fort Mandan

Mandan Villages

Knife R.

To St. Louis

Three Forks

Bozeman Pass

Yellowstone R.

Jefferson R.

Madison R.

Gallatin R.

Lemhi Pass

Snake R.

Continental Divide

LOUISIANA

PURCHASE

POSSESSIONS

here go into all the evidence offered by each group, the affidavits, the government records, the testimony of those who claimed they knew the Bird Woman. But we can and should examine the chief arguments.

Those who believe that Sacajawea died when she was only twenty-three or twenty-four years old base their belief on a few references to "Charbonneau's wife" found in contemporary journals. One of these references is found in the journal of Henry Brackenridge, a Pittsburgh lawyer and writer who was traveling up the Missouri with an expedition in June of 1811. Brackenridge wrote:

We had on board a Frenchman named Charbonneau, with his wife, an Indian woman of the Snake nation, both of whom had accompanied Lewis and Clark to the Pacific and were of great service. The woman, a good creature, of a mild and gentle disposition, greatly attached to the whites, whose manner and dress she tries to imitate, but she had become sickly and longed to revisit her native country; her husband, also, who had spent many years among the Indians, had become weary of a civilized life.

The Snake woman is not named, but many historians think she was Sacajawea. The entry does indicate that Charbonneau and this wife had spent several years among civilized people, probably in the St. Louis region. However, it is generally accepted that the interpreter had several wives. Also, it would not be unlike Charbonneau to try to attract attention by claiming that the woman with him was the noted Bird Woman.

A year and a half later, on December 20, 1812, a Snake woman died at a trading post on the Upper Missouri. John C. Luttig, clerk at the post, reported:

This evening the wife of Charbonneau a Snake squaw died of a putrid fever. She was a good and the best Woman in the fort, aged about 25 years she left a fine infant girl.

Again the woman is not named, but many scholars believe she was Sacajawea. There is, of course, no record of Sacajawea's birth date, though it is generally believed to be about 1789, which would make her twenty-three years old in 1812, or thereabouts. The other Snake girl kidnapped by the Minnetarees is believed to have been some two years older than the Bird Woman, or about twenty-five at this time.

One other reference is quoted. In his notebook for the years 1825 to 1828, Captain Clark listed the names of the members of the expedition, with a brief comment on their present whereabouts. Beside the name of Sacajawea he wrote one word—"Dead." This would seem to be absolute proof that Sacajawea died before that entry was made if it were not that Clark wrote the same word opposite the name of Patrick Gass, who was alive and would live for many years.

Other claims by those who believe 1812 is the date of the Bird Woman's death are that Charbonneau in these years had but one wife, Sacajawea, and one son, Jean Baptiste, as Pomp would be called throughout the remainder of his life. The other group supports its stand by quoting from Captain Clark's journal of the expedition. On November 11, 1804, the officer wrote:

two Squars of the Rock mountains, purchased from the Indians by a frenchman came down

The younger of the two was Sacajawea, the older by two or three years was also the interpreter's wife, given the name Otter Woman in order to have some means of referring to her. It is borne out by many accounts that Charbonneau had a number of wives. He married the last one when he was eighty years old. The men at Fort Clark gave the couple a rousing charivari, at which the old man danced till dawn.

As for the two sons:

In the summer of 1813, Luttig, the clerk at Fort Manuel, came to St. Louis with the baby girl left by the dying Indian woman the previous December. He and Indian women at the post had cared for the baby until spring made it possible for the clerk to come downriver to St. Louis. He was looking for Captain Clark, who had been a friend of the baby's father and even then was probably educating the Frenchman's two sons. Luttig hoped that Clark would tell him what to do with the baby girl, now an orphan, the clerk believed. He had heard that Charbonneau had been killed during an Indian attack near the mouth of the Yellowstone.

Captain Clark, who had been Superintendent of Indian Affairs for some time, was away on government business, so Luttig went to the Orphans' Court and was appointed guardian for "Toussaint, a boy about ten years of age, and the girl, Lizette, about one year old, children of Toussaint Charbonneau."

When Clark returned a few days later and learned of Luttig's visit and its result, he obtained the guardianship papers; Luttig's name was scratched out and the officer's name written in, making Clark the legal guardian of these two children of Charbonneau.

This incident, which is of court records, shows that Charbonneau had a son named after him, probably his firstborn. This is further indicated by an entry in Clark's record of expenses for 1820, where this entry is found: "May 17 To F. Neil for quarter's tuition Toussaint Charbonneau, half Indian boy, $12." So this namesake of old Charbonneau was being educated in 1820. The best estimates of his age make him about seventeen; Baptiste would have been fifteen years and one month old.

So far as has been found, there is no other recorded mention of Toussaint, though the journals of Western trappers sometimes mention a "Tessou" or "Tesson." Since this unidentified half-breed frequently appears at the same place and the same time as does Baptiste, many scholars believe that he was Baptiste's half-brother. For example, both were at Bent's Fort in the spring of 1842, but while old Charbonneau and Baptiste appear in the stories of the early West, Sacajawea is not mentioned.

It is not surprising that historians ignored this exceptional woman for so many years. It was only in the 1960s that they began recognizing the contributions of women of any race. Charbonneau's life is fairly well disclosed: he remained a fur trader and interpreter, wandering over much of the frontier until his death at eighty-one. Whether Sacajawea was with him during any of his travels we cannot know. She must have been alive in 1813 when John Luttig applied to be named guardian of Toussaint and Lizette. The clerk did not ask to be made guardian of Baptiste, although he thought the boy's father was dead. Evidently his mother was alive, and according to Indian custom was the guardian of her son.

During the years immediately following the expedition, some of the journals kept by the two officers and five other members were published. They made little impression on the American public; the brief mentions of Sacajawea were scarcely noticed.

Then, in 1904, the hundredth anniversary of the Louisiana Purchase was to be celebrated by a great exposition in St. Louis. The following year, the centennial of the Lewis and Clark journey was chosen for a similar celebration in Portland, Oregon. In honor of these events, Reuben Gold Thwaites, secretary of the Wisconsin State Historical Society, decided to edit and publish an unabridged edition of the famous captains' journals, with letters and excerpts from other members' records. It took eight large volumes, each in two parts, to contain all this material.

Researchers for the two expositions began to search through

the journals to find material to bolster and enhance their projects. One such worker was Mrs. Eva Emery Dye, who helped with the Portland Lewis and Clark Centennial Exposition. Mrs. Dye was captivated by Sacajawea, the only woman to make that historic journey. She used what little knowledge there was about the Bird Woman and wove a fanciful tale called *The Conquest*, based on the heroine's life. The book became very popular, many readers accepting the entire story as historical fact. But historians knew that it was a novel, and their curiosity was aroused. What were the facts?

Among the interested historians was Dr. Grace Raymond Hebard, a member of the Wyoming State Historical Society, who spent some thirty years tracing the movements of the Shoshone. Another was Dr. Charles A. Eastman, an investigator for the Office of Indian Affairs, engaged to study documents and visit Indian reservations in search of material. A third distinguished investigator was Bruno Louis Zimm, a New York sculptor commissioned to do a statue of the Bird Woman. Determined to have every detail as authentic as possible, Zimm studied the life and character of Snake women. From such research came much that could be proved, much that was vouched for by Indian tribesmen, and much that was based on the customs and traditions of the Shoshones. But there was also a good deal of folklore, legends, and hearsay.

Among the proved items was the fact that Charbonneau had two wives, both kidnapped as young girls by a Minnetaree raiding party. The younger of the two was Sacajawea, while the older girl was given the name Otter Woman. She was the mother of Toussaint, Charbonneau's elder son, who must have been a year or two older than his half-brother.

The old men who were custodians of Comanche history vouched for the story of Sacajawea's years among them. So much of this was built-up detail that about all that is acceptable is the mere fact that Sacajawea spent some of those lost years among the Comanches of the Southwest. These Indians were related to the Shoshones; their language was similar, so it is not to be wondered at that the Bird Woman in her wanderings visited that tribe. As for the details of her stay there, as related in some biographies, these are largely fictional.

Some of the unverified reports seem to point to Sacajawea. For instance, in John C. Frémont's journal of his second expedition to the West in 1843 an interesting incident is related. On July 23, Frémont's party was camped at St. Vrain's Fort on the South Platte River in eastern Colorado. An Indian woman came into camp, leading six well-laden horses. With her were two small children. She told Frémont that her husband, a French trapper, had been killed at nearby Fort Lupton; that she was of the Snake tribe and was on her way to find her people, whom she thought were in the Bear River country. She asked to be allowed to travel with the officers' party and her request was granted. The woman with the two youngsters, whose liveliness amused the explorer, stayed with the party until August 18. They had reached a tributary of the Green River, about two miles from Fort Bridger. There she left the men and went on alone.

This woman may have been Sacajawea, though Frémont does not record her name. The age of the woman, the tribe, the year, and the place fit in with the scant evidence we have. Moreover, it is incredible that *another* Snake woman, who could communicate seemingly with little difficulty with white officers, would be hunting her people at that very time and place. The children, of course, were not hers; they were probably the offspring of the French trapper with whom she had been traveling. This Indian woman introduced Frémont to the yampa root, just as Sacajawea had introduced Captain Clark to it nearly forty years before. The children with her were "pretty little half-breeds, who added much to the liveliness of the camp," just as little Pomp had cheered the adventurers on their long trek to the Pacific. Both of these observations remind one of the Bird Woman.

As interest in Sacajawea grew, stories and anecdotes flourished all over the West. There were reports that Sacajawea had lived not only with the Comanches, but with the Digger Indians in California, with various tribes in Canada, with the Nez Percé, the Blackfeet, and the Bannocks in Idaho. In Utah there is a persistent legend that she spent some time among the Mormon pioneers, marrying a Ute chief. It was said that all United States army officers recognized her as the guide of the Lewis and Clark expedition, that they protected her, and helped her travel across wild and dangerous country.

In Montana it was claimed that Henry Plummer, the notorious sheriff and stage robber, once gave her sacks of flour so she would not leave Virginia City on a certain stage—a stage that was held up that very night. In Colorado it was Joseph A. Slade, described by Mark Twain as an "agent feared a great deal more than the Almighty," who befriended the wanderer. Such stories *prove* nothing, but they do support the belief that an old woman of the Snake tribe wandered throughout the West during the years from about 1820 to some time in the 1860s, when she appeared at Fort Bridger, accepted as the Bird Woman, the companion of Lewis and Clark on the exploring expedition to the Pacific.

Let us take up her story there among her people.

THE LAST JOURNEY

Sacajawea arrived at Fort Bridger sometime before 1860. There she found what she had been searching for, the band of Snake Indians into which she had been born. Their great and good chief, Washakie, was a close relative of her mother. And here was her adopted son, now called Bazil, a subchief of Washakie. He was married and had a family. He welcomed the wanderer as his mother, though he probably could not remember that emotional meeting in the mountains when she had adopted him. He rejoiced in being able to care for his mother after years of thinking she must have died. His story had been kept alive by the tribal singers into whose chants went the history of his people.

Also living at Fort Bridger was a man known as Baptiste, who claimed he was the Bird Woman's son, who had traveled in a cradleboard to the Pacific. He was a dour and uncommunicative fellow, of the same rough character as the Tessou sometimes mentioned in stories of the early West. Bazil, who had seen Pomp only as a papoose, had no way of knowing that this was not that baby grown to manhood. And it seems no one questioned his claim. He was a member of the Snake tribe since he was the son of the so-called Otter Woman, who had been kidnapped by the Minnetarees.

Of course, Sacajawea would know immediately that this was not her beloved Baptiste. But she did not expose him. She would never have so embarrassed a member of her immediate family. But she must have talked to him, begged for news of Baptiste. She may have feared that Toussaint, who had inherited his father's quick

Washakie. A photograph taken around 1882.

temper, had slain his half-brother. What could she do? If she had such suspicions she had no way of proving them. At any rate, this half-breed went on living at Fort Bridger, but Sacajawea did not live with him. She preferred Bazil's family.

Here, among her relatives, Sacajawea was known by many names. She had arrived using the title Porivo, meaning chief or head, and through the years, as she took part in tribal affairs, that name was sometimes used. Her family chose her childhood name of Po-he-nive, or Grass Maiden. Some addressed her as Wadze-Wipe, Lost Woman, due to her years of absence from her people. Government officials used her Minnetaree name, Sacajawea.

At Fort Bridger she lived quietly content. Bazil's tepee and summer bower were some distance from the trading post, which was a famous stopping place for travelers making their way westward. They were coming in ever greater numbers, by wagon or on horseback. Soon they would speed by on shining rails. White people at the post long remembered how the erect, intelligent old woman would ride her horse to the post to sell the moccasins, gloves, and baskets she had made and the animal pelts she had trapped. There she would linger to talk to post employees or visitors.

Sometimes when there was trouble that required wisdom for its solution, she would be summoned to the council of the chiefs and subchiefs. She would sit quietly until Washakie indicated that he wanted her opinion. Then she would rise and speak with such sincerity that her words carried great weight.

The most important of such councils was the famous meeting that resulted in the Bridger Treaty of 1868. Government officials were trying to persuade the Snakes to relinquish their tribal lands and move onto a reservation so the Union Pacific could lay its tracks across this region. If the Indians refused, they could delay the building of the transcontinental railroad.

At this historic meeting, Sacajawea sat among the women beyond the circled chiefs and government officials. Finally Washakie nodded toward her and she stood up. She spoke earnestly, telling her people that the white men were friendly and would give them a home in a place they could choose for themselves. In her wanderings she had seen what happened when the Indian opposed the government. The Indian always lost. But when he cooperated, he received benefits and help. It would be wise to accept the decree from Washington, and to go peaceably to the reservation. The assembled chiefs nodded and the treaty was signed.

The Shoshones chose a region in the Wind River mountains of Wyoming. There Sacajawea was given a small house of her own, though she generally preferred to sleep and to cook out in the open. Here she spent the final years of her life. She was not a hermit. She associated not only with her people, but also with reservation officials, missionaries, and teachers. She was a clever storyteller, and adults as well as children were fascinated by the tales of her adventures, especially that long-ago trip to the Pacific—the wonder of the ocean and the skeleton of the monstrous fish.

She kept physically fit and mentally alert. She was still eager to learn. When she was in her nineties she was working with the reservation schoolteacher, exchanging lessons in Shoshone for lessons in English. But for the most part she lived as her people lived, a Snake squaw on an Indian reservation.

On the morning of April 9, 1884, Bazil found the body of his mother huddled among her blankets. The news spread quickly among the scattered dwellings of the reservation and people came to see what they could do. They found Bazil weeping. They wrapped the small, withered figure in skins, sewed up for her burial. Her body, with her most treasured possessions, was placed on her horse and taken to the reservation headquarters. There her body was placed in a coffin and she was given a white man's burial, as she had said she wanted. The Reverend John Roberts, a Protestant Episcopal minister and the religious adviser for the reservation, inserted in the reservation church register the following:

(Date) April 9, 1884,
(Name) Bazil's mother (Shoshone)
(Age) One hundred.
(Residence) Shoshone Agency.
(Cause of death) Old age.
(Place of burial) Burial ground, Shoshone Agency.
(Signature of clergyman) J. Roberts.

A small group of relatives and friends gathered to watch the interment and hear the simple eulogy. A small wooden slab was placed at the humble grave. This was soon destroyed by the weather. Then a large boulder was set at the head and a smaller stone at the foot of the burial mound. That was all there was for several years.

But as interest in the Bird Woman developed, there was a demand for a suitable marker at her grave, and so a stone shaft was placed where the boulder had been. Then a Cheyenne businessman had a bronze plaque engraved and mounted on this shaft. The plaque reads:

SACAJAWEA
Died, April 9, 1884

A Guide with the
Lewis and Clark Expedition
1805–1806

Identified, 1907 by Rev. J. Roberts,
who officiated at her burial.

It was a marker as much in tune with the windy Wyoming plain

[49]

Monument at the site of Sacajawea's grave.

as was the woman it commemorated. In 1963 the Wyoming Daughters of the American Revolution erected a more dignified gravestone in memory of this outstanding woman.

At one time the Reverend Roberts commented, "I little realized that the heroine we laid to rest, in years to come would become one of the outstanding women of American history." This clearly shows how little attention was paid to Sacajawea during her lifetime. It also explains the reluctance of some writers to admit that they erred in thinking that the mother of Toussaint and Lizette was Sacajawea.

The Bird Woman's service went beyond the purchase of horses, the acting as interpreter. Her quick thinking and forthright action saved precious cargo, warned Captain Lewis of Cameâhwait's planned desertion. She could have been considered a traitor to her people for this betrayal of her brother's plans, but she was loyal to the explorers and saved the expedition and probably the lives of her companions. Her knowledge of which wild plants were edible not only enhanced their meals, but also saved the men from scurvy by providing needed vitamins. Through the entire journey she proved steadfast, dignified, and humble. Sacajawea, Bird Woman, Grass Maiden, Porivo, Lost Woman—by whatever title she is known, it is a mark of honor and respect.

And now, what is known of the men of her family?

Charbonneau, as has been noted, continued to be a fur trader, trapper, and scout. He was last heard of in 1839 when he was eighty-one years old. He visited the office of Joshua Pilcher, then Superintendent of Indian Affairs, and asked to be paid for past services as an interpreter. Pilcher paid him what was due and he left, never to be heard of again.

Little Pomp, that beautiful and promising child, grew up into a handsome, accomplished gentleman. For a few years he lived the free life of the frontier, but in 1823, when he was eighteen, he met

Prince Paul of Württemberg. The Prince was traveling in the American West when he met Baptiste, of whom he became very fond. He persuaded the youth to return to Germany with him, and for the next six years this half-breed Indian lived the life of a European prince. He traveled over Europe and North Africa, learning to speak several languages.

When Baptiste returned to the United States in 1829 he again took up his life as a frontiersman. His personality and education served him well, and he became a very successful dealer in furs. Sometimes he was employed at such posts as Bent's Fort on the Arkansas or St. Vrain's on the South Platte. In 1846 he was a guide for the Mormon Battalion, a group of 500 Mormon men enlisted to help in the struggle for California. Baptiste was a guide on the Battalion's 2,000-mile (3,219-km) march from Iowa Territory to California, the longest infantry march in recorded history.

He became enamored of southern California and settled there. He became the *alcalde* (mayor) of Mission San Luis Rey, which had been established in 1798 to serve a tribe of Shoshones. Later he moved to the gold-mining region, making his home in the booming camp of Auburn in Placer County. Here he became a prosperous and respected businessman.

Nearly twenty years passed and then the old wanderlust took hold. Gold had just been discovered in Montana and Baptiste, with one companion, started for those gold fields. He reached the Owyhee River in eastern Oregon, where he took sick and died. He was sixty-one years old. His obituary was published in Idaho and California papers. The Placer *Herald* of July 7, 1866, gave a review of his services to California during the score of years he spent there.

The Baptiste of Fort Bridger, who is believed to be the young Toussaint, lived for nearly twenty years more, dying in 1885, and was buried on the Shoshone Reservation. Later, when historians

Statue of Sacajawea, with Pomp on her back, in Bismarck, North Dakota.

were trying to unravel the mystery of Sacajawea's life, a search was made for his body. It was hoped that a medal may have been given to old Charbonneau, which, if found on the body, would indicate that this man was really the young Toussaint. But the body was never found and the mystery persists.

The next year Bazil died and was buried in a cave on a stream bank, because the ground was frozen too hard to be dug. Buried with him was a brown leather wallet, which her relatives claimed had belonged to Sacajawea. Later, Bazil's body was exhumed in order to find that wallet and discover what facts the papers in it might reveal. The wallet was there, but its contents had been so damaged by water and soil that they could not be deciphered. Bazil's body was re-interred beside the grave of Sacajawea, with a marker to identify him.

What is left of Sacajawea? What memorials of this historically important woman? Her story in several books, some fictionalized, some inaccurate, and some carefully done; her name on mountain peaks in several northwestern states, peaks so little known they are not listed in *Webster's Geographical Dictionary*, the *American Guide*, or the various state guides published by the Federal Writers' Project; statues in St. Louis, Portland, Bismarck; a mountain peak in the Bitterroots, a riverside park on the Columbia; and some miscellaneous tributes such as murals, and songs.

And always that lonely grave on the high plains of Wyoming.

A NOTE ON
SOURCES

The journals of Lewis and Clark and other members of the expedition to the Pacific in 1804–6 furnish the only universally accepted facts about Sacajawea, the Shoshone woman who accompanied the explorers. I have followed the eight-volume edition of these journals, edited by Reuben Gold Thwaites and published by Dodd, Mead & Co. in 1904–5. Several other editions of the journals have been consulted, specifically that edited by Bernard De Voto and published by Houghton Mifflin in 1953, and David Holloway's *Lewis and Clark and the Crossing of America*, published by the Saturday Review Press in 1974.

For subsequent events in the Shoshone woman's life I have relied largely on the research done by Dr. Grace R. Hebard. See her *Sacajawea*, published by the Arthur L. Clark Co., Glendale, California, in 1933. For the story of her son, Jean Baptiste Charbonneau, see Ann Hafen's article in Dr. LeRoy Hafen's *Mountain Men* (Arthur L. Clark Co.).

Many other journals, historical articles, state histories, and government reports have provided authentic details incorporated into this biography.

INDEX

ABOUT THE
AUTHOR

Olive Burt is the author of over 50 books for young readers on many subjects, most notably in the area of American history, with an emphasis on the American West. A resident, when she is not traveling, of Salt Lake City, Utah, Ms. Burt is a fellow of the Utah Historical Society, a member of the League of Utah Writers, and the recipient of many awards for her work, including a Mystery Writers of America "Edgar" award.